BLACK BOY

RICHARD WRIGHT

BLACK BOY

The vocabulary is based on
Salling/Hvid: English-Danish Basic Dictionary
Weis: Grund- und Aufbauwortschatz, Englisch
Thorndike: The Teacher's Word Book
West: A General Service List

EDITORS
Aage Salling
Erik Hvid *Denmark*

ADVISERS
Otto Weise *Germany*
G. de Groot *The Netherlands*
Erling Rundstrøm *Norway*
Brita af Ekenstam *Sweden*

Cover design: Ib Jørgensen
Illustrations: Oskar Jørgensen

© 1971 by Grafisk Forlag/Aschehoug Dansk Forlag A/S
ISBN Denmark 87-429-7550-6

Printed in Denmark by
Grafisk Institut A/S, Copenhagen

RICHARD WRIGHT

(1908–1960)

is one of the great American story-tellers
of our time. He was born in Mississippi,
where his father was a mill and farm
worker. As his father left his family and
the mother fell ill, the boy was sent to
live with relatives. He went to school in
Jackson, where his aunt taught. After he
left school he worked at several jobs, and
at last became a clerk in a post office. He
started writing early in his life and trav-
elled widely in Mexico, the Gold Coast,
and Europe, where he spent his last years,
in Paris. He writes in a clear and passionate
style which holds the reader's attention
from beginning to end. The present book
is the story of his own youth.

OTHER BOOKS BY RICHARD WRIGHT

Uncle Tom's Children (1938), Native Son
(1940), Black Power (1954), Eight Men
(1961).

fireplace

curtains

flames

I

One winter morning long ago, when I was four years old, I found myself standing before a *fireplace*, warming my hands over the fire, listening to the wind. All morning my mother had been telling me that I must make no noise. And I was angry. In the next room *Granny* lay ill, under the care of a doctor night and day, and I knew that I would be beaten if I did not do as my mother said. I crossed to the window and pushed back the *curtains* – which I had been forbidden to touch – and looked into the street. I was dreaming of running and playing and shouting, but the thought of Granny's old white face made me afraid.

The house was quiet. Behind me my brother – a year younger than I – was playing upon the floor. A bird flew past the window and I shouted.

"You had better be quiet," my brother said.

"You *shut up*," I said.

My mother came into the room and closed the door behind her. She came to me and shook her finger in my face.

"You stop that shouting, you hear!" she said. "You know that Granny is ill and you had better keep quiet."

"I told you so," my brother said.

"You shut up," I told him again.

I walked about the room, trying to think of some-

Granny, grandmother.
shut up, shut your mouth, don't say anything.

thing to do. There was nothing of interest except the fire, and at last I stood before it, looking at the red *flames*.

An idea of a new kind of game came into my mind. Why not throw something into the fire and watch it burn? There was only my picture-book and my mother would beat me if I burnt that. Then what? The *broom!*

Who would care about a few *straws* if I tore them out of the broom and threw them into the fire and watched them burn? Burning straws was a good game, and I took more of them from the broom and threw them into the fire. My brother came to my side.

"Don't do that," he said.

"Why?" I asked.

"You'll burn the whole broom," he said.

"You shut up," I said.

"I'll tell Mother," he said.

"And I'll beat you," I said.

Now I was thinking what the long white curtains would look like if I lit some straws and held them under them. Would I try it? Yes. I pulled some straws from the window and brought the flame to the curtains. My brother shook his head.

"No," he said.

He spoke too late. The flames were eating the curtains. I backed away. The fire came up to the top

straw

broom

8

of the window. I was afraid and looked round for my brother; he was gone. The room was full of smoke. I *made for* the *kitchen;* there was smoke there too. Soon my mother would see the fire and beat me. I had done something wrong, yes, I would run away and never come back. I ran out of the kitchen. Where could I go? Yes, under the house! Nobody would find me there. I *crawled* under the house, so that nobody would find me and beat me.

Soon I heard footsteps on the floor above me. Then I heard shouts. Later the sound of the *fire-engine*. Yes, there was really a fire, a fire like the one I had seen one day burn a house down. I was afraid. I thought of my grandmother lying on her bed with yellow flames in her black hair. Would my mother burn? Would my brother burn? Perhaps everybody in the house would burn! Why had I not thought of that before I set fire to the curtains?

"Richard!" my mother called.

I saw her legs moving outside the house. Her face came down to the ground. She had found me! Her face went away; no, she had not seen me.

fire-engine

---

make for, run towards.
kitchen, room in the house where food is prepared.
crawl, move on hands and feet.

"Richard! The house is on fire. Oh, find my child!"

Yes, the house was on fire, but I had decided not to come out. Then I saw another face looking under the house; it was my father's.

"There he is!" he cried.

"No!" I *screamed.*

"Come here, boy!"

"No!"

"The house is on fire!"

"Leave me alone!"

He crawled to me and took hold of one of my legs.

"Come out of there, you little fool!"

"Let me go!"

He pulled me out. It was over. I would be beaten. I did not care any more. I knew what was coming. The moment his hand left me I jumped up and broke into a wild run. I was caught before I had run ten steps.

I do not remember much of what happened after that, except that no one had died in the fire. Grandfather and an uncle had carried Granny out of the house. But I was beaten so long and so hard that they had to call a doctor, who said I was to stay in bed and be kept quiet if they wanted me to live.

One day my mother told me that we were going to Memphis on a boat, the "Kate Adams". The days until we were going seemed to have no end; each night I went to bed hoping that the next morning would be the great day.

---

scream, cry in a loud and sharp voice.

"How big is the boat?" I asked my mother.
"As big as a mountain," she said.
"Has it got a *whistle*?"

whistle

"Yes."
"Does the whistle blow?"
"Yes."
"When?"
"When the captain wants it to blow."
"Why do they call it the Kate Adams?"
"Because that is the boat's name."
"What *color* is the boat?"
"White."
"How long will we be on the boat?"
"All day and night."
"Will we sleep on the boat?"
"Yes, we'll sleep. Now, be quiet!"

For days I had dreamed about a big white boat
sailing on the water, but when my mother took me
down on the day we were leaving, I saw a small, *dirty*
boat that was not at all like the boat I had seen in

---

color (Amer.) = colour (British English).
dirty, not clean.

my dreams, and when the time had come to go on board I cried and my mother thought that I did not want to go with her to Memphis, and I could not tell her what was the matter. But I felt better when I walked about the boat and looked at the *Negroes* eating, talking, and singing, and when my father took me down into the *engine* room, where I would stay for hours.

In Memphis we lived in a big old house. We had all the four of us only a kitchen and a bedroom. There was space for us to play outside the house, but for days I was afraid to go into the strange city streets alone, and I missed the green, growing things of our old garden.

My father worked at night in a *drugstore*, and we could not make a noise when he was asleep in the daytime. He was the lawgiver in our family and I never laughed when he was present.

One morning my brother and I found a *kitten* that set up a loud meowing. We gave it some food and water, but it still meowed. My father came to the back door and told us to be quiet. We told him it was the kitten that was making the noise and he ordered us to drive it away. We tried to make the kitten leave, but it would not move.

"Get off!" my father shouted.

The kitten just meowed.

Negro, black man or woman.

engine, motor.

drugstore, shop where medicine, soap, perfume and many other things are sold. Often there is also a café in a drugstore.

kitten, baby-cat.

"Kill the thing!" my father exploded. "Do something, get it away from here!"

He went inside. I did not like his shouting. What could I do to make him know? Oh, yes … He had told us to kill the kitten and I would kill it. I knew that he had not really meant me to kill the kitten, but I wanted to show him.

"He told us to kill the kitten," I said to my brother.

"He didn't mean it," my brother said.

"He did, and I'm going to kill it."

My brother ran away. I found a piece of *rope,* and put it round the kitten's neck, took it over a *nail,* and pulled the kitten's feet off the ground. It opened its mouth, and its tongue shot out. I went to find my brother.

nail

rope

"I killed it," I said.

"You did bad," my brother said.

"Now Father can sleep," I said.

"He didn't mean you to kill it," my brother said.

"Then why did he tell me to do it?" I asked.

My brother could not answer; he looked at the kitten hanging down from the nail.

"I'm going to tell," my brother said, running into the house.

I waited, ready to repeat my father's words even though I knew that he had spoken them because he was angry. My mother came up to me. She stopped when she saw the kitten hanging from the rope.

"What have you done?" she asked.

"The kitten was making a noise and Father told me to kill it," I answered.

"You little fool!" she said. "Your father is going to beat you for this."

"But he told me to kill it," I said.

"You shut your mouth."

She took me to my father's bedside and told him what I had done.

"You know better than that!" my father shouted.

"You told me to kill it," I said.

"I told you to drive it away," he said.

"You told me to kill it."

"You get out before I *hit* you," my father shouted, and turned over in bed.

I was happy because I had found a way to tell my father that I didn't like him, and that if he had beaten me, I would never have believed his words again.

But my mother knew what to do. Just before I was to go to bed, she ordered me to go out into the dark and *bury* the kitten.

---

hit, strike.
bury, put in a hole in the ground.

14

"No!" I screamed, feeling that if I went out, something bad would happen to me.

"Get out of here and bury the kitten," she ordered.

"I'm afraid!"

"And wasn't the kitten afraid when you put that rope round its neck?" she asked.

"But it was only a kitten," I said.

"But it was alive," she said. "Can you make it live again?"

"But Father told me to kill it," I said.

My mother hit me on the mouth. "You stop that! You know what he meant. Get out of here and bury the kitten."

I went out into the black night. Though I knew that I had killed the kitten, my mother's words had made it live again in my mind. What would that kitten do to me if I touched it?

"Mother, come and stand by me," I said.

"You didn't stand by that kitten, so why should I stand by you?" she asked.

"I can't touch it," I said.

"Take it down!" she cried.

I took the rope and the kitten fell down with a sound that *echoed* in my mind for many days and nights. Then I buried the kitten and went back to the house, but my mother took my hand and led me to the kitten's *grave* again.

"Shut your eyes and say after me," she said.

I closed my eyes, holding her hand.

---

echo, sound again; you hear an echo when sound is sent back by a hill or a mountain.

grave, hole in the ground where he had buried the kitten.

"Dear God, our Father, forgive me, for I knew not what I was doing . . ."

"Dear God, our Father, forgive me, for I knew not what I was doing," I said.

At first I did not really know what *hunger* meant, but now I began to wake up at night to find hunger standing at my bedside, looking at me with wide open eyes. The hunger I had known before this had been a normal hunger that had made me ask for food, but this new hunger made me angry. When I asked for food, my mother would now give me a cup of tea which would help for a moment or two, but a little later I would feel hunger again. I did not play as much as before, and for the first time in my life I had to stop and think of what was happening to me.

"Mama, I'm hungry," I said one afternoon.

"Jump up and catch a kungry," she said, trying to make me laugh and forget.

"What's a kungry?"

"It's what little boys eat when they get hungry," she said.

"What does it taste like?"

"I don't know."

"Then why do you tell me to catch one?"

"Because you said you were hungry," she said, smiling.

But this made me angry.

"I'm hungry. I want to eat."

"You'll have to wait."

"But I want to eat now."

---

hunger, feeling of pain because you have had no food.

16

"But there's nothing to eat," she told me.

"Why?"

"Just because there's none."

"But I want to eat," I said, beginning to cry.

"You'll have to wait," she said again.

"But why?"

"For God to send some food."

"When is He going to send it?"

"I don't know."

"But I'm hungry."

She looked at me with tears in her eyes.

"Where's your father?" she asked me.

I looked at her. Yes, it was true that my father had not come home to sleep for many days now and I could make as much noise as I wanted. But I had not understood that this would mean that there would be no food.

"I don't know," I said.

"Who brings food into the house?" my mother asked me.

"Papa," I said. "He always brought food."

"Well, your papa isn't here now," she said.

"Where is he?"

"I don't know," she said.

"But I'm hungry," I said.

"You'll have to wait until I get a job and buy food," she said.

My mother at last went to work as a cook and left me and my brother alone in the house each day with a *loaf of bread* and a *pot* of tea.

loaf of bread

teapot

When she came back in the evening she would be tired and would cry a lot. Sometimes she would call us to her and talk to us for hours and tell us that we now had no father, and that we must learn to take care of ourselves. We did not understand what had happened between our father and our mother; whenever we asked why father had left, she would tell us that we were too young to know.

One evening my mother told me that I would have to do the shopping for food. She took me to the *store* at the corner to show me the way. I was proud. The next afternoon I took the *basket* and went down the street towards the store. When I got to the corner, a group of boys *knocked* me *down,* took my basket and the money, and sent me running home in fear. That evening I told my mother what had happened, but she said nothing; she sat down at once, wrote another note, gave me more money, and sent me out to the store again. I walked down the steps and saw the same boys playing down the street. I ran back into the house.

"What's the matter?" my mother asked.

"It's those same boys," I said. "They'll beat me."

"You've got to get over that," she said. "Now, go on."

basket

---

store (Amer.), shop.
knock down, strike hard to make somebody fall.

"I'm afraid," I said.

"Go on," she said. "Now, go on."

I went out of the door and walked quickly down the street.

"There he is!" someone cried.

They came towards me and I broke into a wild run towards home. They knocked me down again, and they took the money out of my hand, gave me a few *slaps*, and sent me home crying. My mother met me at the door.

"They beat me," I said. "They took the money."

"Don't you come in here," my mother said.

"But they're coming after me."

"You just stay where you are," she said. "I'm going to teach you this night to stand up and fight for yourself."

She went into the house and I waited. Then she came out with more money and another note; she also had a long heavy stick.

"Take this money, this note, and this stick," she said. "Go to the store, and if these boys do anything to you, then fight."

"But I'm afraid," I said.

"Don't you come into this house until you have got the things from the store," she said.

"They'll beat me; they'll beat me," I said.

"Then stay in the streets; don't come back here!"

I ran up the steps and tried to get past her into the house. A hard slap came on my face. I stood in the street, crying.

"Please let me wait till tomorrow," I said.

---

slap, a blow with the open hand.

"No," she said. "Go now! If you come back into the house, I'll beat you."

She shut the door. I was alone in the dark street. I would be beaten either in the street or at home. I tried to think. If I were beaten at home, there was nothing I could do about it; but if I were beaten in the streets, I at least had a chance to fight. I took the stick and walked down the street.

"There he is again!" the cry went up.

They came up to me and felt for my hand.

"I'll kill you!" I cried.

They came nearer. I let the stick fly and heard it hit a boy's head. I struck again, hitting another boy.

I fought to knock them down, to kill them. I hit again and again. The boys moved away; they had never seen anyone so *mad*. I stood still and asked them to

---

mad, wild, angry, out of his mind.

come on and fight. They didn't, and I ran after them. They ran home, crying, and their fathers came into the street, and for the first time in my life I shouted at *grown-ups*, telling them that I would give them the same if they touched me. Then I went to the store. On my way back I held the stick in my hand ready for use, but there was not a boy to be seen. That night I won the right to the streets of Memphis.

One summer afternoon – in my sixth year – while I was looking under the doors of a *saloon*, a black man caught hold of my arm and pulled me into the room. I cried and tried to break free of him, afraid of the crowd of men and women, but he would not let me go. He sat me on the *counter*, put his hat upon my head and ordered a drink for me. The crowd shouted with pleasure. Somebody tried to put a cigar in my mouth, but I turned my head.

"How do you feel, sitting there like a man, boy?" a man asked.

"Make him drunk and he'll stop looking in here," somebody said.

"Let us buy him drinks," another said.

Some of my fear left me, as I looked at them. Whisky was set before me.

"Drink it, boy," somebody said.

I shook my head. The man who had pulled me in, put the glass to my mouth. I said no.

---

grown-up, person who is not a child any more.
saloon (Amer.), restaurant where people go to have drinks.
counter, table in a shop.

21

"Drink it, you'll feel good," he said.

I drank. The men and women laughed. The crowd came up to stand around me, asking me to drink. I drank again. My head turned and I laughed. I drank again and again and I ran laughing and shouting among the crowd. As I would pass each man, I would drink out of his glass. Soon I was drunk.

A man called me to him and *whispered* some words

---

whisper, speak in a very low voice.

22

in my ear. He told me he would give me a *nickel* if I went to a woman and said them to her. I told him that I would say them. He gave me the nickel and I ran to the woman and shouted the words. A storm of laughter went up in the saloon.

"Don't teach the boy that," someone said.

"He doesn't know what it is," another said.

From then on, for a penny or a nickel, I would say

---

nickel, a 5-cent piece.

to anyone whatever was whispered to me. I ran from person to person, shouting things that made them roll with laughter.

"Let the boy alone now," someone said.

"It won't hurt him," another said.

"Go home, boy," somebody shouted at me.

They let me go, and I walked along the street, drunk, shouting the things I had learnt in the saloon.

After that, many an evening my mother would find me in the streets, drunk, and take me home and beat me, but the next morning, no sooner had she gone to her job than I would run to the saloon and wait for someone to take me in and buy me a drink. My mother protested to the man who owned the saloon, and he told me not to come in, but the men would buy me drinks anyway. My mother did not know what to do. She beat me and cried over me, telling me that she had to work. At last she sent me and my brother to an old black woman who watched me every moment to keep me from running to the doors of the saloons to beg for whisky. At last I felt I did not want it any more and I forgot the taste of it.

In the afternoon the school children would stop outside the house and play; they would leave their books on the ground and I would turn the pages and ask them what was in them. When I learned to *recognize* certain words, I told my mother that I wanted to learn to read and she helped me. Soon I was able to pick my way through most of the children's books I ran across. This made me want to know about things,

---

recognize, know when you see or hear again what you have seen or heard before.

and when my mother came home from a hard day's work, I would ask her so many questions about what I had heard in the streets that she *refused* to talk to me.

One cold morning my mother called me and told me that, because there was no *coal* in the house, she was taking my brother with her and that I must stay in bed until the coal she had ordered was brought to the house. I went back to sleep, and woke up when somebody rang the bell. I opened the door, and let in the coal-man.

"Are you cold?" he asked.

"Yes," I said.

When I had given him money he said, "How much *change* should I give you?"

"I don't know," I said.

"Don't you know how to count?"

"No, sir," I said.

"Listen and say after me," he said.

He counted to ten and I listened; then he asked me to count alone and I did. He then taught me the words twenty, thirty, forty, etc., then told me to add one, two, three, and so on. In about half an hour's time I had learned to count to a hundred and I was very happy. Long after the coal-man had gone I danced up and down on the bed, counting again and again to a hundred, afraid that I should forget how to do it. When my mother came back I told her to stand still and listen to me. She was very surprised.

---

refuse, say no.
coal, black mineral that burns and gives off heat.
change, small coins given instead of a bigger coin.

I began school at a later age than was usual; my mother had not been able to buy me the clothes to make me look like the other children. The boys of the street took me to school the first day and when I came to the *school grounds* I was *frightened* and wanted to return home. But the boys took my hand and pulled me inside the building. I was still frightened and the other children had to tell the teacher my name and address. I sat listening to the other children *recite,* but could not open my mouth.

On the playground I found myself in a group of older boys and followed them about, listening to their talk. In half an hour I learned more about men and women, boys and girls than anybody had ever told me before, and not in the best language. When I came home, my head was full of new things, but not a single idea from books. I ate my food quickly, took a piece of soap and ran into the street. I wanted to show people all I had learned in school since morning. I went from window to window and wrote in big soap-letters all the words the boys had told me. I had written on nearly all the windows in the street when a woman stopped me and drove me home. That night the woman came to see my mother and told her what I had done, taking her from window to window to show her my writings. My mother wanted to know where I had learned those words and refused to believe me when I said I had learned them at school.

---

school grounds, land belonging to the school, playground.
frightened, afraid.
recite, say aloud what the teacher has asked the children to learn.

pail

My mother got a *pail* of water and a piece of cloth, took me by the hand and led me to the first window.

"Now, wash until that word is gone," she ordered.

People stood around me, asking my mother how I could have learned so much so quickly. I washed windows till I grew blind with *anger*. I cried and asked Mother to let me go, telling her that I would never write such words again; but she did not let me go until the last soap-word had been washed away. Never again did I write words like that; I kept them to myself.

---

anger, the feeling of being angry.

27

My mother fell ill and food became a problem. Hunger was with us always. Sometimes the *neighbors* would feed us, or a dollar would be sent by post from Grandmother. It was winter and I would go out every morning to buy a paper bag full of coal. For a time I stayed away from school to look after my mother, then Granny came to visit us and I returned to school.

At night there were long *discussions* about our going to live with Granny, but nothing came of it, and Granny went home and left us a few dollars. At last we could not pay the *rent* for the rooms we lived in, and my mother went out to find a place where she could send us. She found an *orphan* home, and one morning my mother took me and my brother to the place.

The house was full of children and there was always a lot of noise. The meals were bad and there were only two of them, and if a child did anything bad he was sent to bed without food.

At the beginning my mother came to see us every night, then her visits stopped. I began to wonder if she, like my father, had gone away never to come back. So when she did come, I asked her why she had stayed away so long, and she answered that they had told her that it was not good for us if she came too often. I begged my mother to take me away; she

---

neighbor (Amer.) = neighbour (British English), person living in the next house.

discussion, talk, going over the reasons for and against.

rent, money paid for living in a house.

orphan, child having lost its father and mother.

cried and told me that soon she would take us to Arkansas.

I decided that as soon as night came I would run away. When dinner came I did not go to the table, but hid behind a door. When I heard them eating, I opened the door and ran down the street. Dark was coming and I was afraid. People passed me. Where was I going? I did not know. No, I could not go on. I would go back. But I had walked so far and turned so many corners. Which way led back? I did not know. I was lost.

I stood in the middle of the street and cried. A "white" policeman came up to me and I wondered if he was going to beat me. He asked me what was the matter and I told him that I was trying to find my mother. A crowd gathered and I was asked where I lived. I was too full of fear to cry now. I wanted to tell the "white" policeman that I had run off from an orphan home and that Miss Simon was the head of it, but I was afraid. At last I was taken to the police station where they gave me something to eat. I felt better. Through the window I could see that it was dark. I fell asleep. When I opened my eyes, another policeman was sitting beside me, and before I knew it I had told him that I had run away from an orphan home and that Miss Simon was the head of it.

A few minutes later I was walking beside a policeman towards the home. The policeman led me to the house, and I saw Miss Simon standing on the steps waiting for me. When the policeman had left, I begged her not to beat me, but she took me to an empty room and beat me long and hard. In bed that night I decided to run away again, but they watched me closely.

My mother was told about it and she was frightened.

"Why did you do it?" she asked.

"I don't want to stay here," I said.

"But you must," she said. "You must remember that you have no father. I'm doing all I can."

"I don't want to stay here," I said.

Questions

1. Why was Richard not allowed to make any noise?
2. How did he set fire to the curtains?
3. Where did Richard hide?
4. What did his father do to him when he caught him?
5. Why did Richard cry when he went on board the boat?
6. Why did Richard kill the kitten?
7. What did his mother make him do in the evening?
8. Why had they no food in the house?
9. What happened to Richard on his way to the shop?
10. Why did his mother say that he must go?
11. Why were there no boys in the street when he came back?
12. What did the men in the saloon give Richard?
13. What did Richard's mother do to get him away from the saloon?
14. How did Richard learn to read?
15. What did he learn from the boys in the school-grounds?
16. Why did Richard's mother send the two boys to an orphan home?
17. Why did Richard run away?

2

My mother arrived one afternoon with the news that we were going to live with her sister in Elaine, Arkansas, and that on our way there we would visit Granny in Jackson, Mississippi. I was very happy and ran about to gather my clothes.

I was so *eager* to go that when I stood in the hall I did not even think of saying good-bye to the boys and girls with whom I had eaten and slept and lived for so many weeks. My mother told me to shake hands with them, and I did. In the years to come I was often made to do things other people expected of me though I did not and could not feel what they felt.

In Granny's house lived a *colored* schoolteacher, Ella, a young woman that I liked very much though I was afraid of her. I had long wanted to ask her to tell me about the books that she was always reading, but I dared not. One afternoon I found her alone in the garden, reading.

"Ella," I said, "please tell me what you are reading."

"It's just a book," she said.

"But what's it about?" I asked.

"Your grandmother wouldn't like it if I talked to you about books," she told me.

"I don't care," I said.

"Shhh – you mustn't say things like that."

---

eager, wanting very much.
colored (Amer.) = coloured (British English), not white.

"But I want to know."

"When you grow up, you'll read books and know what's in them," she explained.

"But I want to know now."

She thought a while, then closed the book.

"Come here," she said.

I sat at her feet and looked up at her.

"Once upon a time there was an old, old man . . .", she began in a low voice.

She whispered to me the story of "Bluebeard and His Seven Wives" and I no longer saw the garden, the sunshine, her face, or anything else. As her words fell upon my ears, they became real in a way I had never known before. She told me how Bluebeard had married his seven wives, how he had loved and killed them, how he had hanged them up by their hair in a dark room. The story made the world around me be, live, move; the look of things changed and the world became different. I stopped her all the time to ask her questions. The feelings the story called up in me were never to leave me. When she was about to finish, Granny came out.

"You stop that, you *evil* girl!" she shouted. "I want none of that in my house."

For a moment I did not know what was happening.

"I'm sorry, Mrs Wilson," Ella said. "But he asked me – ."

"He's just a child and you know it," Granny said angrily.

Ella bowed her head and went into the house.

---

evil, bad, wicked.

We were at the *railroad* station with our bags, waiting for the train that would take us to Arkansas, and for the first time I saw there were two lines of people at the *ticket window,* a "white" line and a "black" line. When we were on the train I found that we Negroes were in one part of the train and that the whites were in another.

"Can I go and look at the white *folks?*" I asked my mother.

"You keep quiet," she said.

"But that wouldn't be wrong, would it?"

"Will you keep still!"

"But why can't I?"

I had begun to notice that my mother became

---

railroad (Amer.) = railway (British English).
ticket, piece of paper showing that one has a right to go to a place, by train or bus.
folks, people.

ticket window

TICKETS

angry when I asked her questions about whites and blacks, and I could not quite understand it. I wanted to understand why those two sets of people who lived side by side never touched unless they fought. Now, there was my grandmother... Was she white? Just how white was she? What did the whites think of her whiteness?

"Mama, is Granny white?" I asked as the train rolled through the darkness.

"If you've got eyes, you can see what color she is," my mother said.

"I mean, do the white folks think she's white?"

"Why don't you ask the white folks that?"

"But you know."

"Why should I know?" she asked. "I'm not white."

"Granny looks white," I said. "Then why does she live with us colored folks?"

"Don't you want Granny to live with us?" she asked.

"Yes."

"Then why are you asking?"

"I want to know."

"Doesn't Granny live with us?"

"Yes."

"Isn't that enough?"

"But does she want to live with us?"

"Why didn't you ask Granny that?"

"Did Granny become colored when she married Grandpa?"

"Will you stop asking silly questions!"

"But did she?"

"Granny didn't become colored," my mother said angrily. "She was born the color she is now."

"Why didn't Granny marry a white man?" I asked.

"Because she didn't want to."

"Why don't you want to talk to me?" I asked.

She slapped me, and I cried. Later, she explained that Granny's parents and grandparents had been Irish, Scotch and French, and Negro.

"What was Granny's name before she married Grandpa?"

"Bolden."

"Who gave her that name?"

"The white man who owned her."

"She was a slave?"

"Yes."

"And Bolden was the name of Granny's father?"

"Granny doesn't know who her father was."

"So they just gave her any name?"

"They gave her a name; that's all I know."

"Couldn't Granny find out who her father was?"

"For what, silly?"

"So she could know."

"Know for what?"

"Just to know."

"But for what?"

I could not say. I could not get anywhere.

"Mama, where did Father get his name?"

"From his father."

"And where did the father of my father get his name?"

"Like Granny got hers. From a white man."

"Do they know who he is?"

"I don't know."

"Why don't they find out?"

"For what?" my mother asked.

And I could think of no reason why my father should try to find out who his father's owner was.

"What has Papa got in him?" I asked.

"Some white and some red and some black," she said.

"Indian, white, and Negro?"

"Yes."

"Then what am I?"

"They'll call you a colored man when you grow up," she said. Then she turned to me, smiled and said: "Do you mind, Mr Wright?"

I was angry and I did not answer.

When we arrived in Elaine I saw that Aunt Maggie lived in a house with a *fence* around it. It looked like home and I was glad. Aunt Maggie's husband, Uncle Hoskins, owned a saloon. I begged him to

---

fence, see illustration on page 38.

fence

take me to see it and he promised; but my mother
said no. Well, if I could not see the saloon, I could
at least eat. And there was so much food on Aunt
Maggie's table that I could not believe it was real.
It took me some time to get used to the idea that
there was enough to eat; I felt that if I ate enough
there would not be anything left for another time.
When I first sat down at Aunt Maggie's table, I
could not eat until I had asked:

"Can I eat all I want?"

"Eat as much as you like," said Uncle Hoskins.

I did not believe him. I ate until my *stomach* hurt,
and even then I did not get up from the table.

"Your eyes are bigger than your stomach," my
mother said.

"Let him eat all he wants to and get used to food,"
Uncle Hoskins said.

---

stomach, part of the inside of a person's body that receives the
food.

When *supper* was over I saw that there were many *biscuits* left on the table. I was afraid that there would be no bread for breakfast in the morning, so I took some of the biscuits and hid them about the house, in corners and under beds, until I was sure that there would always be bread in the morning.

Each day Uncle Hoskins went to his saloon in the evening and did not return home until the early hours of the morning. Like my father he slept in the daytime, but my brother and I shouted and *banged* as much as we liked, and he did not seem to care. Often I went into his room while he slept to look at the big revolver that lay near his head. I asked Aunt Maggie why he kept the gun so close to him and she told me that some men had said they would kill him, white men . . .

One morning I woke up to learn that Uncle Hoskins had not come home from the saloon. Aunt Maggie wanted to go to the saloon to see what had happened, but Uncle Hoskins had told her never to go there. The day passed and dinner-time came.

"I'm going to find out if anything has happened," Aunt Maggie said. But she did not go. It grew dark, and still he had not come.

"I hope the white people didn't do anything to him," she said.

Later she went into the bedroom and when she came out she said:

---

supper, evening meal.
biscuit, small hard cake.
bang, make a noise, as when closing a door by pushing it.

"He didn't take his gun. I wonder what could have happened?"

We ate without a word being said. An hour later there was the sound of footsteps outside. Aunt Maggie ran to the door. A tall black boy stood there. He took off his hat.

"Mr Hoskins ... he *done been shot*. Done been shot by a white man," the boy said. "Mrs Hoskins, he dead."

Aunt Maggie cried out, and ran into the street.

"Don't you go to the saloon," the boy called. "They'll kill you if you go there. White folks will kill all his family."

My mother pulled Aunt Maggie back into the house. That night we put all our clothes and things in a farmer's *wagon*, and before *dawn* we were rolling away. We stopped at West Helena, and Aunt Maggie and my mother kept inside the house all day, afraid to be seen in the streets. But at night Aunt Maggie went back to Elaine several times, and she

wagon

---

done been shot (Negro Amer.), has been shot.
dawn, the first light of day.

blackboard

would tell no one except my mother when she was
going.

My mother and Aunt Maggie cooked in the houses
of white folks, and my brother and I were free to
play where we wanted all day. I lived in West
Helena a long time before I returned to school. My
mother got a job in a doctor's house at five dollars
a week, and at once she decided that her sons were
"going to school again." I was happy, but I was
still afraid, and on the first day at school the whole
class laughed at me. I was sent to the *blackboard*
to write my name and address. I knew my name
and address, knew how to write it, knew how to
spell it, but standing at the blackboard with the eyes

of the many girls and boys looking at my back made me go cold inside, and I could not write a single letter.

"Write your name," the teacher called to me.

I took up the white *chalk* and I was about to write when my mind went *blank;* I could not remember my name, not even the first letter.

"Just forget us and write your name and address," the teacher said.

My hand could not move.

"Don't you know your name?" the teacher asked.

I looked at her and could not answer. The teacher rose and came to my side.

"What's your name?" she said.

"Richard," I whispered.

"Richard what?"

"Richard Wright," I said.

"Spell it."

I spelled my name.

"Now write it."

Again I turned to the blackboard and put up my hand but could do nothing. The whole room started to laugh.

"You may go to your seat," the teacher said.

I knew how to write as well as any boy or girl in the classroom, and I could read better than any of them, and I could talk well when I was sure of myself. Then why did strange faces make me go cold and empty?

While sitting in class one day, I was surprised to

---

chalk, white thing you write on a blackboard with.
blank, empty, with nothing in it.

shoulder

hear bells ringing. Soon there was a lot of noise. The boys and girls ran to the windows. The teacher left the room and when she came back she said:

"Everybody can go home."

"Why?"

"The war is over," the teacher said.

I followed the rest of the children into the streets and saw that black and white people were laughing and singing and shouting. I felt afraid as I went through crowds of white people, but my fear left me when I came into my own street and saw smiling black faces. I noticed that many boys and girls were looking at something in the sky; I looked up and saw what seemed to be a little bird.

43

"Look!"

"A *plane*!"

I had never seen a plane.

"It's a bird," I said.

The crowd laughed.

"That's a plane, boy," a man said.

"It's a bird," I said. "I see it."

A man lifted me up on his *shoulder*.

"Boy, remember this," he said. "You're seeing a man fly."

I still did not believe it. It still looked like a bird to me. That night at home Mother told me that men could fly.

Questions

1. Where did Granny live?

2. Who was Ella, and what did she tell Richard?

3. What did Richard not understand about whites and blacks?

4. What colour was Granny?

5. Why did Richard hide the biscuits?

6. What happened to Uncle Hoskins, and why?

7. Why couldn't Richard say or write his name?

8. What did he think that he saw in the sky?

---

plane, see illustration on page 43.

shoulder, see illustration on page 43.

3

Having grown taller and older, I now made friends
with older boys. In the afternoons when school was
over, I would walk down the street, until I would
see one or more of the *gang* standing in a field, or
sitting on somebody's doorstep.

"Hey."

"Have you eaten yet?"

"Yeah, man."

"They say a white man hit a colored man up
north and that the colored man hit the white man,
and nobody did a thing."

"Man for man up there."

"They say they have got houses in New York
forty stories high!"

"Man, I would be afraid of those houses."

"You know, they say that those buildings rock in
the wind."

"No, nigger."

"Yeah, they say they do."

"You think that could be?"

"No! If a building rocked in the wind it'd fall.
Any fool knows that."

We were now big enough for the white boys to
fear us, and both of us, the white boys and the black
boys, began to play our *roles* as white and black as
though we had been born to them and they were in

---

gang, group of persons working together or keeping together.
role, an actor's part in a play; a part played in real life.

our blood. If the white boys came to our side of the *roundhouse* we *stoned* them, and if we happened to find ourselves on their side we were stoned by them.

My mother became too ill to work and I began to do *chores* in the neighbors' houses. My first job was to carry lunches to the men who worked in the roundhouse, for which they gave me 25 cents a week. When the men did not finish their lunches I ate what was left over. Later I got a job in a café carrying wood in my arms to keep the big *stove* going. I got a dollar a week for this work.

One morning a shouting voice woke me.

"Richard! Richard!"

I rolled out of bed. My brother came running into the room.

"Richard! You'd better come and see Mama. She is very ill," he said.

I ran into my mother's room and saw her lying upon her bed, her eyes open. She was very still.

"Mama!" I called.

She did not answer or turn her head. I went forward to touch her, but drew back, afraid that she was dead.

stove

---

roundhouse, a building for locomotives.
stone, throw stones at.
chore, small job.

"Mama!" I called again, not able to understand that she could not answer.

My brother and I looked at each other; we did not know what to do.

"We had better get somebody," I said.

I ran into the hall and called a neighbor. A tall, black woman came out of a door.

"Please, won't you come and see my mama? She won't talk. We can't wake her up. She's very ill," I told her.

She followed me.

"Mrs Wright!" she called to my mother.

My mother lay still. The woman felt her hands.

"She isn't dead," she said. "But she's ill, all right. I had better get some more of the neighbors."

Five or six women came and my brother and I waited in the hall while they took her clothes off and put her to bed.

One of the women asked if there was any money in the house. I did not know. They looked around and found a dollar or two and sent for a doctor. The doctor arrived. Yes, he told us, my mother was very ill. Someone must be with her day and night, and she must have medicine. Where was her husband? I told him the story and he shook his head.

"She'll need all the help she can get," the doctor said. "She cannot talk and she will have to be fed."

I wrote a letter to Granny, asking her to come and help us. The neighbors looked after my mother day and night, gave us food and washed our clothes. What if Granny did not come? Though I was a child, I could no longer feel as a child. I was glad that my mother was not dead, but she would be ill

47

for a very long time. When Granny came, I left everything to her.

I wrote letters for Granny to her eight children, asking for money with which "to take Ella and her two little children to our home". Money came, and my mother was taken to the train in an *ambulance*.

ambulance

We rode to Jackson, and Mother was put to bed. Doctors came and went. Night and day I could hear *groans* from her room. We thought that she would die at any moment.

Aunt Maggie, who had left us some time before, came back from Detroit. Aunt Cleo came from Chicago. Uncle Clark came from Mississippi. Uncle Edward came from Carters. Uncle Charles came from Mobile, Alabama, Uncle Thomas from Hazelhurst Mississippi. I heard them talking about "what is to become of her children", and I felt afraid, and at night my sleep was filled with dreams. One night I found myself standing in the yard. The moon was shining. Suddenly I felt that someone was holding my hand. I looked and saw one of my uncles. He was speaking to me in a low, gentle voice.

---

groans, deep sounds of one in pain.

"What's the matter, son?"

I looked at him, trying to understand what he was saying.

"Richard, what are you doing?"

I could not answer. It seemed that I could not wake up. He shook me. I came to myself.

"Where are we going?" I asked him.

"You were walking in your sleep," he said.

One evening my brother and I were called into the front room where all the uncles and aunts were gathered.

"Richard," said an uncle, "Aunt Maggie is going to take your brother to Detroit and send him to school."

I waited. Who was going to take me?

"Now, where would you like to go?"

"Anywhere," I said.

"Any of us is willing to take you."

Quickly I thought which of them lived nearest to Jackson. Uncle Clark lived in Greenwood, which was only a few miles away.

"I'd like to live with Uncle Clark, since he's close to the home here," I said.

"Is that what you really want?"

"Yes, sir."

"All right. I'll take you back with me and send you to school. Tomorrow we'll go and buy clothes".

Uncle Clark took me to school. The first half of the day passed well enough. The books were easy, and I felt that I could keep up. But my fear was still in me. Were the boys easy to get on with? How hard did they fight?

At noon I went into the playground and a group of boys came up to me and looked at me from head to foot.

"Where are you from?" a boy asked.

"Jackson," I answered.

"Why don't they make people nice to look at in Jackson?" he asked.

"You're not too nice to look at yourself."

"Oh!"

"Oh!"

"You hear what he told him?"

"I don't want to fight," I said. "But if you want to, I'll fight."

"Hard, are you?"

"As hard as you."

The boy came close. Our faces were quite near each other.

"You think I'm afraid of you, don't you?" he asked.

Somebody pushed the boy into me. I pushed him back.

"Don't push me!" the boy said.

"Then keep away!" I said.

They pushed again, and I hit him with my right hand on the mouth. The crowd shouted and pushed us. I fought like a dog. I knew that if I did not win, I'd have to fight a new boy every day. The bell rang.

In the classroom the boys asked me questions about myself. I was someone worth knowing. When the bell rang for school to be over, I was set to fight again; but the boy was not to be seen.

No sooner had I won my right to the school

grounds than a new fear arose. One evening before bedtime, I was sitting in the front room, reading. Uncle Clark was at his table, drawing, and Aunt Jody was *sewing*. The doorbell rang, and Aunt Jody answered it. The *visitor* was one of the neighbors, Mr Burden. I rose and shook his hand.

"Well, son," Mr Burden told me, "it's certainly nice to see another boy in this house."

"Is there another boy here?" I asked.

"My son was here," said Mr Burden. "We used to live in this house. But he's gone now."

"How old is he?"

"He was about your age," Mr Burden said.

"Where did he go?" I asked.

"He's dead," Mr Burden said.

"Oh," I said.

I had not understood him. Nobody said anything for a long time.

"Do you sleep in there?" he asked, pointing to my room.

"Yes, sir."

"That's where my boy slept," he said.

"In there?" I asked.

"Yes, right in there."

"On that bed?" I asked.

"Yes, that was his bed. When I heard you were coming, I gave your uncle that bed for you," he explained.

After Mr Burden had gone, I went to Uncle Clark.

---

sew, work with a needle and thread.
visitor, person coming to see you, guest.

"I'm afraid to sleep in there," I told him.

"Why? Because a boy died in there?"

"Yes, sir."

"But, son, that's nothing to be afraid of."

"I know, but I am afraid."

"You'll get over it."

"But can't I sleep somewhere else?"

"There's nowhere else for you to sleep."

"May I sleep here, on the sofa?"

"No," Aunt Jody said.

I went into the dark room and got into bed; it seemed to me that I touched the dead boy. I put the covers over my face. I did not sleep that night, and my eyes were red the next morning.

"Didn't you sleep well?" Uncle Clark asked me.

"I can't sleep in that room," I said.

"You slept in it before you heard of that boy who died in there, didn't you?" Aunt Jody asked me.

"Yes, ma'am."

"Then why can't you sleep in it now?"

"I'm afraid."

"You stop being a baby," she told me.

The next night was the same; fear kept me from sleeping. After Uncle Clark and Aunt Jody had gone to bed, I rose and crept into the front room and slept on the sofa. I woke in the morning to find Uncle Clark shaking me.

"Why are you doing this?"

"I'm afraid to sleep in there."

"You go back into that room and sleep tonight," he told me. "You must get over this thing."

"Uncle Clark, send me back to Jackson," I said.

"You're not happy here?"

"No, sir," I answered.

"And you really want to go back?"

"Yes, sir."

"Things will not be easy for you at home. There's not much money for food," he said.

"I want to be where my mother is," I said.

"But what about school?"

"I don't care."

"All right," he said. "I'll send you home on Saturday."

I was glad to see my mother. She was much better, though still in bed. The doctor had said she must have another operation. Uncle Edward came from Carters to take my mother to Clarksdale for the operation; at the last moment I said I wanted to go with them. We said very little during the trip, and when we came to the doctor's room I was sure I should never see her again. He took her inside. We waited. Hours later the doctor came out of the door.

"How's my mother?"

"Fine!" he said.

"Can I see her now?"

"No, not now."

Uncle Edward had gone out to get a room and a *nurse* for my mother. He returned with an ambulance and two men. They entered the doctor's room and brought out my mother.

"Why are they taking Mama away?"

"There is no room in the hospital for colored people, and this is the way we have to do it."

---

nurse, woman who looks after sick people.

They lifted my mother into the ambulance and drove away. I knew she had gone out of my life. I could feel it.

She remained in bed ten years, growing better little by little, but never really well. The family had got together all the money they could get, and there was no more to do anything with.

Questions

1. What did Richard talk with the other boys about?

2. What happened to Richard's mother?

3. What happened to the two brothers? Where did they go?

4. Why did the boy not want to fight again?

5. Why did Richard not want to sleep in his room?

6. Why did he go back to his mother?

walnut

Aunt Addie, Granny's youngest child, was the
teacher of the religious school, and that was where
I was sent. From the first day we were bitter ene-
mies. She had not taught before, and it seemed to
me that she did not like to have a member of her
family in her class. At the end of the first week open
war broke out between us.

One afternoon she rose from her table and walked
down to my desk.

"Look at that floor!" she said.

I looked and saw little bits of *walnut* on the clean
floor.

"I don't know anything about that," I said.

"You know better than to eat in the classroom."

"I haven't been eating," I said.

"Don't lie!"

"Aunt Addie, my walnuts are here in my pocket."

"I'm Miss Wilson!"

I looked at her. She had told me to call her Miss Wilson in the classroom, and for the most part I had done so.

"I'm sorry," I said.

"Richard, get up!"

I did not move. I had not eaten the walnuts, and I did not want to be beaten for it. I hoped that the boy in front of me would save me, since he was the one to have done it.

"I asked you to get up!" she shouted.

"I haven't done anything," I said.

She struck me. I moved away.

"Stand still, boy!"

I stood still.

"Hold out your hand."

I held out my hand, and she struck me until the hand was red.

"Put down your hand and go to your seat," she said.

I sat down. I was sure of one thing: I would not be beaten by her again. I knew I had been beaten for a reason that was not right. All afternoon I was wondering how I could get out of the school.

The moment Aunt Addie came into the house, she called me into the kitchen. When I entered I saw that she was holding a stick.

"You're not going to beat me again!" I told her.

"You beat me for throwing walnuts on the floor!
But I didn't do it!"

"Then who did?"

I told her the name of the boy.

"Why didn't you tell me before?" she asked.

"I don't want to tell tales on other people."

"So you lied?"

I could not talk.

"Hold out your hand."

"You're not going to beat me."

"I'm going to beat you for lying."

For a moment she waited, then she struck at me
with the stick and I fell into a corner. She was upon
me. I jumped up, and opened a *drawer;* it fell to
the floor with a loud noise. I took a *knife* and held
it up.

drawer

knife

"Now, I told you to stop!" I shouted.

"You put down that knife!"

"Leave me alone, or I'll cut you!"

She stood still, then she made up her mind and came at me. I hit out with the knife and she took my hand and tried to take the knife. I threw my right leg behind her, and we fell to the floor. She was stronger than I, and she was still trying to get the knife.

"Leave me alone!" I shouted.

"Give me that knife, boy!"

"I'll kill you! I'll kill you if you don't leave me alone!"

Granny came running.

"Addie! What are you doing?"

"He's got a knife!" she said. "Make him put it down!"

My mother came to the door.

"Richard, put down that knife!" she shouted.

"I won't! I'm not going to let her beat me."

"Addie! Leave the boy alone," my mother said.

Aunt Addie rose slowly, her eyes on the knife, then she turned and walked out of the kitchen.

"Richard, give me that knife," my mother said.

I tried to explain, but they would not listen.

Granny was the oldest member of her church, and in the house we had *prayers* in the morning and in the evening, at the breakfast table and at the dinner table. I did not go to church as often as she wanted

---

prayer, words in which you ask God for help.

me to; I said I had no time and had to *study*. Every day I went to my room, and tried to pray, but it was no use. I could not pray. So to pass the time in my room I took the Bible, *pencil* and paper and tried to write *hymns*. But that was no good either.

One day during my hour of prayer I happened to remember some Indian history books I had read the year before. Yes, I knew what I would do; I would write a story about the Indians ... But what about them? Well, an Indian girl ... I wrote of an Indian woman, beautiful and good, who sat on the side of a river, waiting ... and not knowing how to go on, I decided that the girl had to die. She rose slowly and walked into the dark water and walked on until the water reached her neck; then it covered her. Not a sound came from her, not even in dying.

I read it over and saw that it was no good. But I had never in my life done anything like it; I had made something no matter how bad it was; and it was mine ... Now, who could I show it to? I decided to read it to a young woman who lived next door. When I had finished she smiled at me in a strange way.

"What's that for?" she asked.

"Nothing," I said.

"But why did you write it?"

"I just wanted to."

"Where did you get the idea?"

pencil

---

study, do my homework for school.
hymn, song used in church.

"Oh, I don't know. I just thought it up."

"What are you going to do with it?"

"Nothing."

I never forgot the look of surprise on the young woman's face.

Questions

1. Who was Aunt Addie?

2. Why did she beat Richard?

3. How did he stop her from beating him a second time?

4. What did Richard do in his room? What was his story about?

5. Who did he show the story to?

straw hat

I went to school, feeling that what was important was not so much learning things as getting into another world of people. The first day at the Jim Hill school I walked into the school yard wearing a new *straw hat*. I hoped nobody would notice me, but knew that sooner or later somebody would find out that I was a new boy. A black boy ran past me, threw the straw hat to the ground, and shouted:

"Straw hat!"

I picked up the hat and another ran past, pushed my hat off my head, and shouted:

"Straw hat!"

Again I picked up my hat and waited. The cry spread. Boys gathered around me, pointing, crying:

"Straw hat! Straw hat!"

"Where are you from?" a boy asked me.

"None of your business," I said.

"Now, you be careful, or I'll cut you down," he said.

"I'll say what I please."

The boy picked up a small stone, put it on his shoulder and walked close up to me.

I waited a moment, then I pushed the stone from his shoulder, bent down, put my arms round his legs and brought him down. I jumped upon him and started beating him. Then I was pulled up, and another boy began to fight me.

"Don't hit my brother!" he shouted.

Both of them closed in on me. I felt I was hit on the back of my head. I turned round and saw a stone rolling away, and I felt blood coming down my back. I bent down and picked up some stones. The boys backed away. One of them turned and ran. I threw a stone and hit him in the middle of his back. I ran after the other, while the boys crowded round me. Suddenly they all moved away. I saw a woman teacher coming down to me.

"Was it you who threw that stone?" she asked.

"Two boys were fighting me," I told her.

"Come," she said.

I was taken to a room with the two brothers.

"Are these the boys?"

"Both of them fought me, and they tore up my new hat."

"He hit me first," one of them shouted.

"You're lying!" I cried back.

The teacher ordered me to sit down; I did, but

kept my eyes on the two brothers. The teacher took them out of the room and I sat still until she came back.

She asked me my name and sent me to a room. For a reason I don't know they put me in the fifth *grade*. Would they find out that I did not belong there? I sat and waited. When I was asked my age I called it out, and they said I could stay.

I studied day and night and in two weeks I was put in the sixth grade. The family had not thought it possible. How could a bad, bad boy do that?

I was now with boys and girls who were studying, fighting, talking. I knew I was in the middle of a world that I had to meet and fight when I grew up. Suddenly I could see the *future* before me, as much of a future as there is for a black boy in Mississippi.

I was *reserved* with the boys and girls at school because I did not want them to ask questions about my home, and to guess how much I was being kept out of the world in which they lived. Every day at noon I would follow the boys into the corner store and stand against the wall and watch them eat *sandwiches,* and when they would ask me: "Why don't you eat a lunch?" I would answer: "Ah, I'm not hungry at noon, ever."

 sandwich

---

grade (Amer.), group of children in school of the same age, class, form.

future, time to come.

reserved, keeping myself to myself.

I now saw a world come to life before my eyes because I could go out and watch it, though that meant not going home when school was over. Had I gone home to have a meal, Granny would not have allowed me to go out again. With my books over my shoulder I would go out with my friends into the woods, to the river, to business streets, to the movies when we could get in without paying. I was happy to be free and didn't care if I had to go without food for twelve hours.

In my class was a tall, black boy who was very bright in his studies. It was he who found out that I was always hungry and told me a way to make money.

"You can't sit in school all day and not eat," he said.

"What am I going to eat?" I asked.

"Why don't you do like me?"

"What do you do?"

"I sell papers."

"I'd like to sell papers because I could read them. I can't find things to read."

"You too?"

"What do you mean?" I asked.

"That's why I sell papers. I like to read them and that's the only way I can get hold of them," he explained.

I followed him home and he gave me a *copy* of the newspaper.

---

copy, thing made to be just like another; the newspaper is sent out in half a million copies every day.

"Hurry up and start selling them. I'd like to talk to you about the stories."

I promised that I would order some the same night. I walked home reading, lifting my eyes now and then in order not to run into anybody.

The papers arrived and I soon sold a number of them to people who bought them more because they knew me than because they wanted to read. When I returned home in the evening I would go to my room and read. The stories were not very good, but I wanted to believe them; to me they became the door to another world.

One day I came to the house of a friend of the family.

"You know, son," he said, "I do like to see you make a little money every week."

"Thank you, sir," I said.

"But tell me, who told you to sell these papers?"

"Nobody."

"Where do you get them from?"

"Chicago."

"Do you ever read them?"

"I read the stories in the magazine part. But I never read the newspaper."

"Did a white man ask you to sell these papers?"

"No, sir. Why do you ask?"

He did not answer. He was sitting outside the house. He got up slowly.

"Wait here a minute. I want to show you something."

He entered the house, and came back with a copy of the newspaper. He handed it to me.

"Well, just look at this. Take your time and tell me what you think."

I took the paper from him, sat down and read. I turned the pages and read things that were so *anti*-Negro that I felt like cold water being poured down my back.

"Do you like that?" he asked me.

"No, sir."

"Do you see what you are doing?"

"I didn't know."

"Are you going to sell those papers now?"

"No, sir. Never again."

I walked home with the papers under my arm, feel-

---

anti-, against.

ing that some Negro might jump upon me from behind the corner of a house.

The father of the boy who told me to sell the papers also found out about them, and told his son not to sell them. One day he asked me:

"Are you still selling those papers?"

"Oh, no. I don't have time," I said, but I didn't look at him.

"Nor do I," he said. "I'm too busy."

I studied very hard. At the beginning of the school *term* I read my books through and only looked in them again when in class. I did all my mathematics a long time before I was asked to. Then during school hours, when I was not asked to recite, I read stories, or dreamed about cities I had never seen and about people I had never met.

I came in from school one afternoon and Aunt Addie met me in the hall.

"Go *upstairs* and say goodbye to Grandpa," she said.

"What's happened?"

She did not answer. I ran upstairs and met Uncle Clark, who had come from Greenwood. Granny caught my hand.

"Come and say goodbye to Grandpa."

She led me to Grandpa's room; he was lying on the bed, looking as well as he ever looked. His eyes were open, but he was so still that I did not know if he was dead or alive.

"Papa, here's Richard," Granny whispered.

---

term, one of the three parts of a school year.
upstairs, up to the second floor.

Grandpa looked at me.

"Goodbye, Grandpa," I whispered.

"Goodbye, son," he said. "Be happy, for God has picked out my s-s-ea . . . in h-heaven . . ."

His voice died. I had not understood what he had said and I wondered if I should ask him to say it again. But Granny took my hand and led me from the room.

"Granny, what did Grandpa say? I didn't quite hear him."

"Shut up. Death is in the house."

"I just wanted to know," I said.

She looked at me.

"He said that God had picked out his seat in heaven," she said.

When I woke up the next morning my mother told me that Grandpa had "gone home".

My clothes were becoming so worn that I did not like to go to school in them. Many of the boys in the class were wearing their first *long-pants suits*. I decided to have it out with Granny; I would tell her that if she did not let me work on Saturdays I would leave home. But when I tried to speak to her, she would not listen. I followed her about the house. Her answer was no and no and no.

"Then I'll leave school," I said.

"Do as you like. I don't care."

"I'll go away from here and you'll never hear from me."

"No, you won't."

"How can I ever learn enough to get a job?" I

said. I showed her my clothes. "Look, I won't go to school like this. I'm not asking you for money or to do anything. I only want to work!"

"I have nothing to do with whether you go to school or not," she said. "If you are too proud to ask God for help, I can't help you."

"I'm going to get a job anyway."

"Then you can't live here."

"Then I'll leave," I said.

"You won't leave."

"I'll leave this minute."

I ran to my room, and began packing my things. I did not have a penny, but I was going to leave. She came to the door.

"You little *fool!* Put down that bag!"

"I'm going where I can work."

She took the bag out of my hands. "All right," she said. "If you want to go to *hell,* then go. God will forgive me, but he won't forgive you."

She ran away from the door. Now I was dead to Granny and Aunt Addie, but my mother rose and came over to me and kissed me.

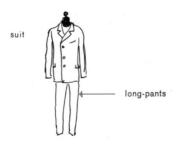

suit

long-pants

---

fool, person who does not think before he acts, stupid person.

hell, the place where bad people are said to go after death.

Questions

1. What did the boys do when they saw Richard's new straw hat?

2. What did the teacher do?

3. Which grade did they put him in?

4. Why did he not have any lunch?

5. What did Richard do to make money? Who told him how to?

6. What did the friend of the family tell Richard?

7. What did Richard do when he had got his school books?

8. What happened to Grandpa?

9. Why did Richard want to leave home?

6

brick   barrow

Summer. Bright hot days. Hunger. Will I be able
to enter school in September? Reading. Looking for
jobs. Hopes of going north. But what would become
of my mother if I left her? Doubt. Fear.

Word came that a *brickyard* wanted men and I
went to find out. I walked into the yard and came
to a *barrow* full of new bricks. I could not even
lift it.

Later I found that they wanted a water boy. I
ran to the office and got the job. I walked in the hot
sun, carrying a big pail from one gang of black men
to another for a dollar a day.

"Water!"

And somebody would call out:

"Here, boy!"

Almost falling down with hunger I would carry
the pail around, and at the end of the week the
money would go into the endless *expenses* at home.

---

brickyard, factory where bricks are made for building
houses.
expenses, sums of money paid out.

Later I got a job in the yard that paid a dollar and a half a day. I went between the walls of new bricks and picked up those which had turned out bad, and took them away in a barrow.

School opened again. I went to classes without books for a month, then I got a job working mornings and evenings for three dollars a week.

One long afternoon I took some paper and told myself I would write a story, but what would the story be about? At last I found out. I finished it in three days and then wondered what to do with it.

The Negro newspaper of the town! That's it ... I sailed into the office and put the story under the nose of the *boss*.

"What is that?" he asked.

"A story," I said.

"All right. I'll read it."

He pushed the papers back on his table and looked at me.

"But I want you to read it now," I said.

"I'll read this and let you know about it to-morrow," he said.

"Give me the story," I said.

He turned from me, took up the papers and read some of it.

"Won't you come in tomorrow?" he asked. "I'll have it finished then."

"All right," I said. "I'll come back tomorrow."

The next afternoon, on my way to work, I stepped into the office.

"Where is my story?" I asked.

---

boss, chief, man in charge.

"It has been printed," he said.

"How much money will I get?" I asked.

"We can't pay you for it."

"But you sell papers for money," I said.

"Look, you're just starting. This story will put your name before our readers. Now, that's something," he said.

"But if the story is good enough to sell to your readers, then you ought to give me some of the money you get from it."

He laughed.

"I'm going to give you something that's better than money. I'll give you a chance to learn to write."

I was pleased, but still I didn't like it.

"What are you doing this summer?"

"Nothing."

"Then come to see me before you take another job," he said. "And write some more stories."

A few days later my friends in the class came to me with copies of the newspaper in their hands.

"Did you really write that story?" they asked me.

"Yes."

"Why?"

"Because I wanted to."

"Where did you get it from?"

"I made it up."

"But what are they printing it for?"

"So people can read it."

"Who told you to do that?"

"Nobody."

"Then why did you do it?"

"Because I wanted to!" I said again.

They were sure it was not true what I told them. We had never learned to write stories at school.

At home it was the same thing. Granny came into my room early one morning and sat down on my bed.

"Richard, what is this you're putting in the papers?"

"A story."

"About what?"

"It's just a story, Granny."

"But they tell me it has been in three times."

"It's the same story. It's in three parts."

"But what is it about?"

"It's a story I just made up."

"Then it's a lie," she said.

"Oh, Christ," I said.

"You must get out of the house if you say such things," she said.

"Granny, please ... I'm sorry. But it's hard to

74

tell you about the story. You see, Granny, everybody knows that the story isn't true, but ..."

"Then why write it?"

"Because people might want to read it."

My mother was also troubled.

"Son, you should not do such things. Suppose they wanted you to teach here in Jackson, and they found out that you had been writing stories."

I could not answer her.

"I'll be all right, Mama," I said.

Uncle Tom didn't like the story, and Aunt Addie said it was a sin to use the words I had put in it.

In the end I was so angry that I refused to talk about the story. Had I known what would happen I would certainly not have wanted to write it.

I dreamed of going north and writing books, stories. To me the North was all that I had not felt or seen. I was wise enough not to hope to become rich. I knew that I lived in a country where a black man could not do all he wanted. Yet I felt I had to go somewhere and do something to pay up for being alive. I was beginning to dream dreams that the state had said were wrong, that the schools had said were *taboo*. My friends at school thought I was doing something that was wrong but they were not able to express it.

---

taboo, not allowed.

Questions

1. Where did Richard get a job?
2. What did he do with his story?
3. What did the newspaper pay him for it?
4. What did his friends at school say? What did Granny say?
5. Why did he dream of going north?

7

Summer again. The old problem of hunting for a job. I told the woman for whom I was working, a Mrs Bibbs, that I wanted a job that would pay me enough money to buy clothes and books for the next school year. She took the matter up with her husband, who worked in a *sawmill*.

"So you want to work in the mill?"

"Yes, sir."

He came to me and put his hands under my arms and lifted me from the floor.

"You're too light for our work," he said.

But I did not leave the room; my standing still there was a way of asking him to think it over again, telling him that I wanted to try for a job in his mill. "All right," he said. "Come to the mill in the morning. I'll see what I can do."

I was at the mill in the morning, and saw the men lifting heavy *logs*.

"Watch out!" somebody shouted.

I looked around and saw a black man pointing above my head. I looked up. A log was swinging towards me. I ran away. The black man came to my side.

"What do you want here, boy?"

"I'm looking for a job."

"I wouldn't try for this if I were you." He held up

---

sawmill, factory where logs are cut up into boards and planks.

his right hand from which three fingers were missing. "See?"

I left.

Empty days. Long days. Bright hot days. I spent the mornings hunting for jobs and I read in the afternoons.

One day I went to the office of the Negro newspaper, but there was no work for me. At last I returned to my job at Mrs Bibb's house, and bought my schoolbooks.

The work in the ninth – my last year at school – was light; and during part of the year the teacher made me *take over*. It was even said that if I was good, it would be possible for me to teach in the city school system.

During that winter my brother came home from Chicago; I was glad to see him, but it was not long before I felt that the family showed him more love than they had ever shown me.

The school year ended. I was chosen to speak for my class. One morning the *principal* called me to his office.

"Well, Richard Wright, here's your *speech*," he said and pushed some papers across his table.

"What speech?" I asked as I picked up the papers.

"The speech you're going to say on the night of *graduation*," he said.

---

take over, do his work for him.

principal (Amer.), head of a school, headmaster.

speech, words spoken (or written down to be spoken).

graduation, leaving school after passing an exam (verb: *graduate*).

"But, professor, I've written my speech already,"
I said.

He laughed. "Listen, boy. You're going to speak
to both white and colored people that night. What
can you alone think of saying to them?"

"I know that I'm only a boy, professor. But the
people come to hear the students, and I won't make
a speech that you've written."

He leaned back in his chair and looked at me in
surprise.

"You know we've never had a boy in this school
like you before," he said. "You've had your way
around here, I don't know how. But, listen, you take
this speech and say it. I know what's best for you.
I have seen many a boy and girl leave this school,
and none of them was too proud to recite a speech
I wrote for them."

"Professor, I'm going to say my own speech that night," I said.

He got angry. "Suppose you don't graduate."

"I have passed my examinations," I said.

"Look, mister," he shot at me, "I'm the man who says who passes at this school."

"Then I don't graduate," I said.

I turned to leave.

"Say, you. Come here." he called.

I turned and looked at him; he was smiling at me.

"You know, I'm glad I talked to you," he said. "I thought I was going to place you in the school system, teaching, but now I don't think that you will fit."

"Look, professor, I may never get a chance to go to school again," I said. "But I like to do things right."

"What do you mean?"

"I've no money. I'm going to work, and this *diploma* isn't going to help me much in life. I'm not bitter about it. But I'm just not going to do things this way."

"Have you talked to anybody about this?"

"No, why?"

"Are you sure?"

"This is the first I've heard of it, professor."

"You haven't talked to any white people about this?"

"No, sir!"

Now I began to understand; the man was afraid for his job.

---

diploma, paper saying that you have passed your exam.

"Now, if you do as I say, I'll help you to go to *college*."

"I want to learn, professor," I told him. "But there are some things I don't want to know."

"Goodbye," he said.

I went home. I had been talking to a "bought" man who had tried to "buy" me. That night Griggs, a boy who had gone through many classes with me, came to the house.

"Look, Dick, you're throwing away your future here in Jackson," he said. "Go to the principal, talk to him, take his speech, and say it. I'm saying the one he wrote. So why can't you? What can you lose?"

"No," I said.

"Why?"

"I know very little, but my speech is going to show that," I said.

"Then they won't take you on as a teacher."

"Who said I was going to teach?" I asked.

He left. Two days later Uncle Tom came to me. I knew that the principal had called him in.

"I hear that the principal wants you to say a speech which you've refused to say," he said.

"Yes, sir. That's right," I said.

"May I read the speech you've written?"

"Certainly," I said.

"And may I see the one the principal wrote?"

I gave him the principal's speech, too. He went to his room to read them both. I sat quiet, waiting. He returned.

---

college, school for young people of 17 to 22 years of age.

"The principal's speech is the better speech," he said.

"Yes. But why did they ask me to write a speech if I can't say it?"

"Would you let me work on your speech?" he said.

"No, sir!"

"Now, look, Richard, this is your future ..."

"Uncle Tom, I don't want to talk about this with you."

He left. The principal's speech was clearer than mine, but it said nothing, mine was not so clear but it said what I wanted to say. What could I do?

Griggs came to my house every day and we went off into the woods to *practise*. Day in and day out we spoke to the trees. At last I could have said my speech in my sleep.

My friends in the class had heard what had happened and said:

"Richard, you are a fool; if they had known they would never have asked you to write a speech."

I asked them to shut up, and in the end the principal had to order them to leave me alone for fear that I would just walk out.

On the night of graduation I was nervous. I got up and my speech rolled out. When my voice stopped, a few people clapped their hands. I did not care if they liked it or not. A few of my friends shook hands with me before I left the hall. Somebody asked me to a party, but I did not go. I did not want to see any of them again. I walked home.

---

practise, do a thing over and over again to learn it.

Questions

1. Why did the man not like Richard to work in the sawmill?

2. Why did Richard not want to take the speech written by the principal?

3. Why did the principal say that Richard might not pass?

4. Why did the principal ask him if he had told any white people?

5. Why did Richard and Griggs go into the woods?

6. Was his own speech a good one?

8

It was important for me now to find work, and I
accepted the first offer, a job as a *porter* in a store
that sold clothes to Negroes *on credit*. The shop was
always full of black men and women who paid any
price the white man asked.

One morning while I was cleaning windows, the
boss and his son drove up in their car. A black woman sat between them. They got out and half kicked
and half pulled the woman ʻinto the store. White
people passed and looked on without saying a word.
A white policeman watched from the corner, but he
made no move. After a moment I heard cries coming
from a room in the store; later the woman walked
out, crying, her clothes torn. When she was in the
street, the policeman went up to her, said she was
drunk, called a police car and had her taken away.

When I went into the store, the boss and his son
were washing their hands. They looked at me and
laughed. There was blood on the floor.

"Boy, that's what we do to niggers when they
don't pay," the boss said.

His son looked at me.

"Here, have a cigarette," he said.

Not knowing what to do, I took it. He lit it for
me. This was as much as to say that even if they

---

accept, say yes to.

porter, doorkeeper, man carrying heavy things for other
people.

on credit, so that they could pay later.

had beaten the black woman, they would not beat me if I knew enough to keep my mouth shut.

"Yes, sir," I said.

After they had gone, I sat on a box and looked at the floor until the cigarette went out.

The store owned a *bicycle* which I used when I *delivered* parcels. One day I had a *puncture* on my way back. I walked along the hot road, leading the bicycle beside me.

A car came up to me.

"What's the matter there, boy?" a white man called.

I told him that my bicycle was broken and that I was walking back to town.

"That's too bad," he said. "Hop on the *running board*."

He stopped the car. I held the bicycle with one hand and held on to the car with the other.

"All right?"

deliver, hand over.
puncture, hole made in a bicycle wheel.

"Yes, sir."

The car started. It was full of young white men. They were drinking.

"Want a drink, boy?"

"Oh, no!" I said.

I had hardly said the words when I felt something hard hit me between the eyes. It was an empty whisky *bottle*. I saw stars, and fell off the car on top of the bicycle. The car stopped and the white men came out and stood over me.

"Nigger, haven't you learned to say 'sir' to a white man yet?"

I got on my feet.

"He's got enough," said one.

"You want to come back to town, nigger?"

"I want to walk," I said.

Before they got back into the car they said:

"You ought to be glad that it was us you met, because if you said that to some other white man, you might be a dead nigger now."

I hated the way they treated Negroes in the clothes store, and they saw it, and sent me away.

I had a number of small jobs for short *periods*, but was told one day by a friend that the only Negro *cinema* wanted a boy to take tickets at the door. The owner accepted me at once, and the next day I began taking tickets. The boss said:

"Now, look, I don't know who is *honest* here and

---

bottle, see illustration on page 85.
period, time.
cinema, house where films are shown.
honest, an honest person does not lie or steal.

who isn't. But if you are honest, then the rest must be honest too. All tickets will pass through your hands. Nobody can steal if you don't steal."

During the first afternoon the Negro girl in the ticket office watched me and I knew she was trying to find out what I was up to.

When I had taken a ticket from a cinema-goer I dropped it into a box. Sometimes the boss would go to the ticket window and look at numbers and then look at the number of the ticket I had just dropped in the box. After a few days he began to watch me from across the street, and at last he stayed away for long periods.

While I was eating in a café near-by one night, a Negro walked in and sat beside me.

"Hello, Richard," he said.

"Hello," I said. "I don't think I know you."

"But I know you," he said.

"How do you know me?" I asked.

"I'm Tel's friend," he said, naming the girl who sold the tickets at the cinema.

I looked at him. Was he telling me the truth?

"We start tonight," he said.

"What?" I asked.

"Don't be afraid. The boss knows you are honest. He has gone to see some friends. Somebody is watching him and if he starts back to the cinema they'll *phone* us," he said.

I could not eat my food.

"It'll work in this way," he explained. "A man will come to you and ask for a cigarette. You give

---

phone, telephone.

him five tickets that you take out of the box, see? We'll give you the signal when to start. The man'll give the tickets to Tel; she'll sell them again at once. *You get it?*"

I did not answer. I knew that if I were caught I would be taken away by the police.

You get it? do you understand?

"Are you with us?"

I still did not answer. He rose and put his hand on my shoulder and left. Anything might happen, but I was used to that.

I took the tickets. I waited.

The man I had met in the café came through the door and put a ticket in my hand.

"There's a crowd at the ticket office," he said. "Take ten, not five. Start with this one."

Well, here goes, I thought. He gave me the ticket and sat looking at the film. After a moment another black man came up to me.

"Got a cigarette?"

I gave him the tickets. He went out to the ticket office and I saw him give the tickets to the girl. She smiled at me and I went back inside. A few moments later the same tickets were handed to me by other cinema-goers.

We worked it for a week and after the money was divided into four parts, I had fifty dollars. I tried to tell Tel's friend that maybe I would leave, but he got very angry.

I went through another week. Late one night I decided to make that week the last. I broke into the neighbor's house and stole his gun. I found two boys who I knew would come with me, and we broke into a store and stole *cans* of fruit which we sold to res-

cans

taurants. I bought clothes, shoes, and a bag, and hid the things at home. Saturday night came, and I sent word to the boss that I was ill. Uncle Tom was in his room. Granny and Aunt Addie were at church. My brother was sleeping. I packed my bag, and went to my mother.

"Mama, I'm going away," I whispered.

"Oh, no," she said.

"I've got to, Mamma. I can't live in this way."

"You're not running away from something you've done?"

"I'll send for you, Mama. I'll be all right."

"Take care of yourself. And send for me quickly. I'm not happy here. I'm sorry for all these long years. But I could not have helped it."

I kissed her and she cried.

"Be quiet, Mama. I'm all right."

I went out the back way and walked half a mile to the station. I bought my ticket, then went back to the cinema. Yes, the boss was there, taking tickets himself. I returned to the station and waited for my train.

Well, it's life, I told myself. I'll see what I can make of it . . .

An hour later I was on my way to the North, to a land where I could live with a little less fear.

Questions

1. Where did Richard find a job?

2. What did they do to the black woman?

3. Who came up when Richard had got a puncture?

4. What did the young men offer to do?

5. Why did they throw a bottle at his head?

6. What was his job at the cinema?

7. What happened in the café?

8. How did they steal the money?

9. How did Richard leave the town?

9

I arrived in Memphis on a cold November Sunday morning. After walking through several streets I saw a big house with a sign in the window: Rooms. I walked up the steps and was about to ring the bell when I saw a big Negro woman looking at me through the window.

"Come here, boy," she called.

I looked at her a moment, then stepped into a warm hall.

She said, "I'm Mrs Moss."

I told her my name.

"We take in *roomers* to *help out*. We are just simple people. You can call this home if you want to. The rent is three dollars."

I accepted and she showed me the room.

"You ran off, didn't you?"

I looked at her in surprise.

"How did you know?"

"Boy, you are like an open book," she said. "I know things. You drink?"

"Oh, no, ma'am."

"Just wanted to know. You can drink here if you like. You can bring your girl here too. Only be a good boy."

I sat on the bed and looked at her. Here in this bad street I had met the warmest, most friendly person I had ever known.

---

roomer (Amer.), person living in a rented room in a house.
help out, make enough money.

eye-glasses

One summer morning I was washing a pair of *eye-glasses* in the factory where I worked. The machines were working around me. It was near noon and I was thinking of lunch. Mr Olin, the white foreman under whom I worked, came up to me.

"Boy, how's it going?" he asked.

"Oh, fine, sir!" I answered.

"Say, Richard, do you believe that I'm your friend?"

I knew that all white men in the South thought themselves the friends of niggers. While thinking of an answer that would say nothing, I smiled.

"I mean," he went on, "do you think I'm your friend?"

"Well," I answered. "I hope you are."

"I am," he said.

I went on with my work.

"I want to tell you something," he said.

"Yes, sir," I said.

"We like you round here; we don't want you to get hurt."

"Yes, sir," I said. "What's wrong?"

He lit a cigarette. "Do you know Harrison?"

He was speaking of a boy of about my own age who worked across the street for another factory.

"Yes, sir," I said. "I know him."

"Well, be careful. He's after you."

"After me? For what?"

"I don't know. What have you done to him?"

I forgot what I was doing. My eyes were upon

Mr Olin's face trying to make out what he meant. I did not trust the white man, nor did I trust Harrison. Who was my friend: the white man or the black boy?

"Well, you had better look out. A little while ago I went down to have a drink and Harrison was waiting for you at the door with a knife in his hand. Said he was going to get you."

"I've got to see that boy and talk to him," I said.

"You had better not," Mr Olin said. "You had better let some of us white boys talk to him. I'll take care of it."

At noon I went across the street and found Harrison sitting on a box inside the door. He was having lunch. As I came up to him, he put his hand in his pocket and looked at me.

"Say, Harrison, what's all this about?" I asked, standing four feet from him.

He looked at me a long time and didn't answer.

"I haven't done anything to you," I said.

"And I haven't got anything against you," he answered.

"But Mr Olin said that you came over this morning, looking for me with a knife."

"Oh, no," he said. "I haven't been in your factory all day."

"Then what did Mr Olin mean?" I asked.

"I thought you were looking for me," Harrison explained. "Mr Olin came over here this morning and said you were going to kill me. He said you were angry because I had said something about you. But I have said nothing about you." He got up.

"Look here, don't believe what Mr Olin says."

"I see now," Harrison said. "He was trying to make us kill each other. But why should he do that?"

"I suppose it's fun for white men to see niggers fight," I said.

At one o'clock I went back to the factory. Mr Olin was waiting for me.

"Did you see that Harrison nigger?" he asked.

"No, sir," I lied.

"Well, he still has that knife for you. Did you buy a knife?"

"No, sir," I answered.

"Do you want to use mine?" he asked.

He put an open knife very near my hand. I put it in my pocket.

I was afraid to look at him; if I had looked at him I would have had to tell him that I knew what he was trying to do. But I said nothing. He was my boss.

In the afternoon I stole a few minutes to run across the street to talk to Harrison. He told me that Mr Olin had telephoned his boss and had told him to tell Harrison that I had planned to wait for him at 6 o'clock and kill him. We told ourselves again and again that we did not believe the white men; yet deep down in us there was a fear that it might be true.

"I wish they would leave us alone," I said.

"Me too," Harrison said.

"There are a million black boys who could do our jobs," I said. "They wouldn't care if we killed each other."

"I know it," Harrison said.

One morning a few days later Mr Olin and a group of white men came to me and asked me if

I was willing to fight Harrison with *gloves*. I told them I was not afraid of Harrison, but I did not want to fight him and did not know how to box. I could feel that they knew that I no longer believed them.

When I left the factory that night, Harrison shouted at me. I waited and he ran up to me. Did he want to cut me? We smiled at each other.

"Did they ask you to fight me with gloves?" Harrison asked.

"Yes," I told him. "But I didn't promise."

"They want us to fight for five dollars each," he said. "Man, if I had five dollars, I could *pay down* on a new suit."

"I don't want to," I said. "Why do a thing like that for white men?"

"To get five dollars."

I was watching Harrison and he was watching me. Did he really want to fight me for some reason of his own? He came up to me and I stepped away. "I need that money," he said.

"I don't," I said.

For another week the white men in both factories asked us to fight. Again Harrison called to me one evening as I was on my way home.

"Come on and fight," he said.

"I don't want to. Now they know that we know what they tried to do to us."

"So let's get the money. You can use five dollars, can't you?"

---

pay down, pay part of the price (and say you will pay the rest later).

glove

coin

"Yes."

"Then let's fight for them."

"I'd feel like a dog."

"To them both of us are dogs."

"All right," I said. "I'll fight."

The fight took place one Saturday afternoon. Each white man who came to see it dropped a *coin* in a hat on the floor. Only white men were allowed in. As the gloves were put on my hands, I looked at Harrison. What was going on in his head?

We began and at once I knew that I could not

pretend to fight. I didn't know enough about boxing to do that, nor did Harrison.

The white men sat smoking and shouting dirty words at us.

"Hit him!"

"Oh, fight, niggers!"

I struck at Harrison with my left, and he landed high on my head, and before I knew it, I had landed a hard right on his mouth and blood came. Harrison shot a blow at my nose. The fight was on, was on against our will. I hit harder, and the harder I fought the harder Harrison fought. The anger we felt for having been made to do this ran into our eyes, and went into the blows we threw at each other. When we were on the point of falling, the white men stopped the fight.

I could not look at Harrison. I hated him and I hated myself. I took the five dollars in my hand and ran home. Harrison and I did not speak to each other after that day. The white men tried to make us fight again, but we said no. I felt I had done something that was not clean, and which I could never forget.

---

pretend to fight, do as if I were fighting.

Questions

1. How did Richard find a room to live in in Memphis?

2. Where did he work?

3. What did the white man say about the other black boy?

4. Where did Richard find Harrison?

5. What had the white man really wanted to make the two black boys do?

6. Why did Harrison want to fight?

7. What was the fight like?

8. What did Richard feel after the fight?

There was a *library* near the river, but I knew that Negroes were not allowed to read the books. I had gone there several times to get books for white men on the job. Which of them would help me to get books? I thought of one after the other and at last decided to speak to a man most of the white men did not like because he was an Irish Catholic.

"I want to ask you something," I whispered to him one day.

"What is it?"

"I want to read. I can't get books from the library. Will you let me use your card?"

"My card is full most of the time."

"I see," I said.

"What book do you want?"

"A book by *H. L. Mencken.*"

"Which one?"

"I don't know."

"Well, I'll think out something. But don't mention this to any other white men."

"I understand," I said. "I won't say a word."

A few days later he called me to him. "I've got a card in my wife's name; here's mine."

"Thank you, sir."

That afternoon I wrote a note to the library asking for "books by H. L. Mencken" and signed the white

---

H. L. Mencken, great American journalist, and writer of political and social works.

library

man's name. I entered the library as I had always done when I had gone there to get books for white people.

"What do you want, boy?"

I handed in the note.

"What books by Mencken does he want?"

"I don't know, ma'am."

"Who gave you this card?"

"Mr Falk," I said.

"Where is he?"

"He is at work. I've been in here for him before."

"I remember," the woman said. "But he never wrote notes like this before."

"You can call him up, ma'am," I said.

"You're not using these books, are you?"

"Oh, no, ma'am, I can't read."

I knew that I had won. I got the books and went out of the library. And that night in my room I began to read. Why did he write like that? And how did one write like that? What was this ... Yes, this man was fighting, fighting with words. Could words be used to fight with? Then maybe I could do the same thing. It was morning before I stopped and I went to work, but I kept thinking of what I had read.

I went to the library again ... and again. The first novel I read was Sinclair Lewis's "Main Street". It made me see my boss in a different light. Now I felt closer to him, I felt now that I knew him and his narrow life, and this only because I had read a book about a man called George F. Babbitt. Every book that I read made me see and feel things in a different way. But I could not help feeling that the white men around me knew that I was becoming different too.

That winter my mother and brother came, and we got a place to live. I began to eat warm food and found that I could read faster. My brother got a job and we began to save money for the trip north. I told none of the white men about my plans, for I felt that they would change towards me if I did.

Aunt Maggie came to see us in Memphis, and this formed a *basis* for our plans. We talked and talked. It was impossible for all four of us to go at once; we did not have enough money. And if we waited until we had, we saw that we should never be able to go. We at last decided that Aunt Maggie and I would go first, though it was winter. Why wait until next week or month? If we were going, why not go at once?

When I told the boss, he turned round in his chair and gave me a long look.

"Chicago?" he said.

"Yes, sir."

"Boy, you won't like it up there."

"Well, I have to go where my family is, sir."

"It's cold up there."

"Yes, sir. They say it is."

"You think you'll do any better up there?"

"I don't know, sir."

"You seem to have been getting along all right down here."

"Yes, sir. If it wasn't for my mother's going, I'd stay here and work."

---

basis, what something rests upon.

"How are you going to act up there?"

"Just as I do down here, sir."

"Would you speak to a white girl up there?"

"Oh, no, sir. I'll act there just as I do here."

"Oh, no, you won't. You'll change. Niggers change when they go north."

I wanted to tell him that that was why I was going, but I did not.

I went to the post office for the last time. When I was back in the factory, I washed my hands, put on my hat and looked at the men who were working late. Mr Falk, to whom I had given back the library card, gave me a smile, and I walked to the *elevator* and rode down.

"You're lucky," said Shorty, the elevator boy.

I stepped out of the elevator into the street, half expecting somebody to call me back and tell me that it was a dream, that I was not leaving.

This was the culture from which I sprang. This was the fear from which I fled.

ELEVATOR

Questions

1. How did Richard get into the library?

2. What did he do to borrow books there?

3. What effect did reading have on Richard?

4. Who came to live with him?

5. What did they plan to do when Aunt Maggie came to see them?

6. How did he get away from his job?